The Great Fire of London

Sarah Blackmore

Published in association with The Basic Skills Agency

Hodder & Stoughton

A MEMBER OF THE HODDER HEADLINE GROUP

Acknowledgements

Cover: Stuart William

Illustrations: Sally Michel

Photos: Mary Evans Picture Library

Every effort has been made to trace copyright holders of material reproduced in this book. Any rights not acknowledged will be acknowledged in subsequent printings if notice is given to the publisher.

Orders; please contact Bookpoint Ltd, 39 Milton Park, Abingdon, Oxon OX14 4TD. Telephone: (44) 01235 400414, Fax: (44) 01235 400454. Lines are open from 9.00–6.00, Monday to Saturday, with a 24 hour message answering service.
Email address: orders@bookpoint.co.uk

British Library Cataloguing in Publication Data
A catalogue record for this title is available from the British Library

ISBN 0 340 77642 0

First published 2000
Impression number   10 9 8 7 6 5 4 3 2 1
Year   2005 2004 2003 2002 2001 2000

Copyright © 1999 NTC/Contemporary Publishing Group, Inc.

Adapted for the Livewire series by Sarah Blackmore

Typeset by GreenGate Publishing Services, Tonbridge, Kent.
Printed in Great Britain for Hodder and Stoughton Educational, a division of Hodder Headline Plc, 338 Euston Road, London NW1 3BH, by Redwood Books, Trowbridge, Wilts

Contents

1 Fire Breaks Out

It was 2 September 1666.
The time was just before midnight.
A fire broke out in a house in London.
The house was made of wood.
Just like many other houses at that time.

It is thought that the fire started
in a baker's shop in Paddington.
The shop belonged to a man called
Thomas Fraynor.
He was the King's baker.

The baker and his family
were sleeping upstairs.
The smoke and flames woke them up.

They had to escape
but there was only one way out.
The baker rushed to the upstairs window.
He opened it and crawled out.
His family followed him.
They crawled along a gutter
to the house next door.

The baker and his family were safe –
but not everybody got out safely.

A girl who worked for the baker
also tried to get out of the window.
She was afraid of heights.
She slipped and fell.
The fall killed her.

2　The Fire Spreads

The fire spread to other houses.
It was made worse by a strong east wind
that carried it across the street.

The wooden houses burned quickly.
The fire blazed through a pub
called the Star Inn.

Old London Bridge 1616.

The blazing fire spread
through the streets of London.
It set light to wooden warehouses
and sheds next to the River Thames.
It blazed through the night
and was still burning by the next morning.

The fire had destroyed houses,
churches, pubs and factories.
It had started to blaze across London Bridge.

3 London in Panic

The people of London were shocked.
They ran out of their houses in panic.
They tried to take their things with them.

They carried them on their heads or backs.
Some put their things into boats on the river.

Their city was on fire.
It was burning to the ground.

The heat of the fire was very strong.
It was so hot that the pavements glowed.
Sparks were flying everywhere.
The strong wind blew them around.

After the first day,
there was thick, yellow smoke.
It spread over the city.
It was so thick that it blocked out the sun.

4 St. Paul's Cathedral

The fire blazed on.
It crept closer and closer
to St. Paul's Cathedral.
It was not long before St. Paul's
was surrounded by fire.

The roof lit up first.
The heat of the fire
melted the lead on the roof.
The molten lead ran down the walls.

The destruction of old St. Paul's cathedral.

The heat was so strong that
it made stones explode out of the walls.
They flew everywhere.
Huge chunks of stone fell into the streets.
No one could get past.

In the end the roof of St. Paul's fell down.
The shock waves could be felt
all over London.

Many people had thought
that St. Paul's would be safe.
They did not think
that the fire would destroy it.

There were a lot of bookshops near St. Paul's.
The booksellers had moved their books
into the cathedral.
They thought they would be safe there.

They were wrong.
As the fire blazed it set light to the books.
Thousands of books went up in flames.
The burning pages were carried off
by the strong wind.
Some landed miles away from London.
Piles of books were still burning
a week after the fire was out.

5 Fighting the Fire

Water was needed to fight the fire.
The River Thames was nearby.
There was a huge water wheel
that lifted water from the river
to the level of the street.
However, the wheel was made of wood.
It caught fire and was destroyed.

The people of London had to use buckets.
They filled the buckets at the river.
They made a line and passed the buckets
from one person to the next.

The fire was too big.
They could not get enough water
using buckets.

The Lord Mayor of London tried to organise
the fire-fighting.
He told people to pull down buildings
in front of the fire.
He hoped that this would make a fire-break
and would stop the fire.
A fire-break is a strip of land which is
kept clear to help stop the spread of fire.
A strong wind spread the flames
before the fire-break was finished.

The Lord Mayor's plan had failed.
The fire blazed on.

6 The King's Plan

The King, Charles II, tried to help.
He had an idea to make a better fire-break.
He decided to blow up buildings
using gunpowder.

This plan failed as well.
The fire-break did not work.
The fire blazed on.

King Charles used gunpowder
from the Tower of London.
This was where the gunpowder was stored.
If the fire reached the Tower,
it would reach the gunpowder.
There was enough gunpowder
to blow up half of London.

Gunpowder was not the only thing in the Tower.
London's goldsmiths needed a safe place
for their gold.
They moved it to the Tower.
They thought the Tower would be safe.

The fire was creeping closer and closer
to the Tower.
The heat was really strong.
The goldsmiths knew that the heat
would melt the gold.

They worked together to save the gold.
They made a line.
They passed the gold from hand to hand.
They put it into boats on the River Thames.
The boats carried the gold to safety.

People worked really hard to fight the fire.
They wanted to save the Tower.

King Charles and his brother
went through the streets.
They gave gold coins to people
fighting the fire.
On the third day, King Charles and his brother
helped with the buckets.
The people of London saved the Tower
but were not able to put the fire out.

7 Over at Last

The fire blazed for five days.
Five dreadful days.
Then at last it burned itself out.

About 13,000 houses were burned.
Almost 400 streets were wiped out.
Nearly 100 churches and some hospitals
were destroyed.

How many people were killed?
Records show that only six people died
in the Great Fire.

The fire had destroyed so much
but it also did some good.
A new law was passed.
It said that buildings should be made
of brick or stone.
Hand pumps were to be used
instead of the wooden buckets.
A volunteer fire service was started.

The fire also stopped a disease that had killed
many people.
Fleas, carried by rats, had spread a disease
called the Black Death.
The fire killed off the rats and their fleas
and put an end to the Black Death in London.